Usborne
Phonics Readers
Ted in a red bed

Phil Roxbee Cox
Illustrated by Stephen Cartwright
Edited by Jenny Tyler

Language consultant: Marlynne Grant
BSc, CertEd, MEdPsych, PhD, AFBPs, CPsychol

There is a little yellow duck to spot in every picture.

First published in 2006 by Usborne Publishing Ltd., Usborne House, 83-85 Saffron Hill, London EC1N 8RT, England. www.usborne.com
Copyright © 2006, 1999 Usborne Publishing Ltd.

Ted likes to shop.

Ted stops. Ted hops.
Ted smiles a big smile.

3

"I like this bed," thinks Ted.

"I like red wood. Red wood is good."

"I want to see more."

He goes into the store.

"Try the red bed," says Fred.

"Oh, yes," says Ted.

Ted slips his feet under the sheet.

He flops on the pillow.

The pillow is yellow.

"I need this bed, Fred!" grins Ted.

"It is a nice price," smiles Fred.

8

Now it's Ted's bed, not Fred's bed.

Ted feels sleepy.
Ted falls asleep.

Ted has a dream.

He bobs down a stream.

Ted has a dream.

He bobs on a wave

into a cave.

11

Ted has a dream.

He can
fly in the sky!

12

Ted has a dream.
He is back by the stream.

13

Ted wakes up with a snore.

He's not in the store any more.

Ted is home. His bed is home too.

"This red bed must be a magic red bed!"

Usborne
Phonics Readers
Ted's shed

Phil Roxbee Cox

Illustrated by Stephen Cartwright

Edited by Jenny Tyler

Language consultant: Marlynne Grant
BSc, CertEd, MEdPsych, PhD, AFBPs, CPsychol

There is a little yellow duck to find on every page.

First published in 2006 by Usborne Publishing Ltd., Usborne House, 83-85 Saffron Hill, London EC1N 8RT, England. www.usborne.com
Copyright © 2006, 2001 Usborne Publishing Ltd.

Meet Ted. Ted likes red.

Even Ted's shed is a red shed.

Today, Ted's bed goes into the shed.

"What are you doing, Ted?" asks Fred.

"Wait and see,"
says Ted.

Up on his stool, Ted gets down his tools.

5

He puts in a paw,
and pulls out
a saw.

It's time to
start sawing.

Ted looks at
his drawing.

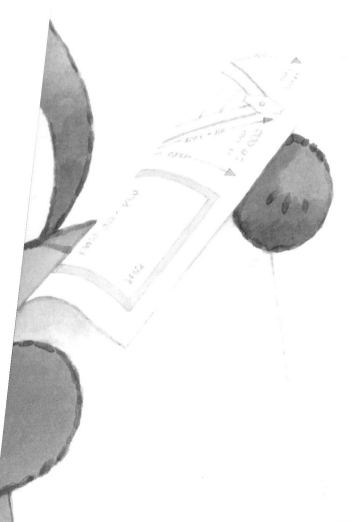

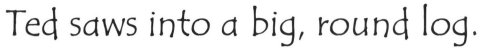

Ted saws into a big, round log.

"What are you up to?"
asks Pup the dog.

7   8

"Wait and see," says Ted.

He saws off a big, round slice.
"This wood is good. This slice is nice."

9

Now Ted saws off slice after slice.

Look who's watching – a pair of mice!

Next, Ted hunts for his jar of nails.

Look, the mice
have the nails in
their tails!

The jar
is empty...

...apart from
a snail.

Ted and his team work on in the sun.

They huff...
...and they puff...
...but it's lots of fun!

13   14

Fred and Pup ask, "What's this all about?"

"Just wait and see!" the others shout.

Did you spot Ted's clever plan?

His red shed is now a caravan!

Usborne
Phonics Readers
Toad makes a road

Phil Roxbee Cox
Illustrated by Stephen Cartwright
Edited by Jenny Tyler

Language consultant: Marlynne Grant
BSc, CertEd, MEdPsych, PhD, AFBPs, CPsychol

There is a little yellow duck to find on every page.

First published in 2006 by Usborne Publishing Ltd., Usborne House, 83-85 Saffron Hill, London EC1N 8RT, England. www.usborne.com
Copyright © 2006, 2000 Usborne Publishing Ltd.

Toad hops happily.
She has a new house on the hill.

"My new house is best," she boasts.

3

Toad waits and waits for the truck to bring her things.

Time ticks on...

She's out of luck.
Where is that truck?

Is the truck stuck?

Toad hops down
the hill.

She's in luck.
There's the truck.

"I can't get up the hill. The load will spill."

There's no track for the truck.

So, Toad brings her things up the hill.

Toad is tired.
   With one last hop
      she flops into bed...

Next day, Toad eats toast
"Today is my party!"

But only Billy the goat gets up the hill.

"It's far too steep,
except for me
or a sheep."

"What you need
is a road, Toad."

"If I need a road, then I'll make a road!" says Toad.

"But toads can't make roads," says Billy. "That's silly."

"Wait and see!" says Toad.

Toad clears a track.

She lays black, sticky tar.

TOAD'S ROAD
TO TOAD'S HOUSE.

ALL WELCOME.

Then she rolls it flat.

Toad's road is ready.

15

Now Toad's in luck.
Here comes the truck!

16

Usborne
Phonics Readers
Mouse moves house

Phil Roxbee Cox

Illustrated by Stephen Cartwright

Edited by Jenny Tyler

Language consultant: Marlynne Grant

BSc, CertEd, MEdPsych, PhD, AFBPs, CPsychol

There is a little yellow duck to find on every page.

First published in 2006 by Usborne Publishing Ltd., Usborne House, 83-85 Saffron Hill, London EC1N 8RT, England. www.usborne.com

Copyright © 2006, 2002 Usborne Publishing Ltd.

Mack the mouse is
moving house.

Mack packs his backpack.

Now Mack packs his plates.

Here is Mack's
friend Jack.

Together, Mack and
Jack pack and pack.

CRACK! Look out, Jack!

Jack packs Mack's
nick-nacks in a
black sack.

It's time to pack
the pictures.

...then they stop for a cheesy snack.

Mack and Jack pack...

and they stack... Now Mack is all packed.

"That's that!" says Jack.

11

Jack helps Mack
put his backpack
on his back.

"Run!"
shouts Jack.
"It's a cat."

Mack opens his door and walks out onto the floor.

But Mack stays out.

He chats with the cat.

"Come here, Jack. Meet my friend Fat Cat."

Mack the mouse
is moving house
on Fat Cat's back!

Usborne
Phonics Readers
Hen's pens

Phil Roxbee Cox

Illustrated by Stephen Cartwright

Edited by Jenny Tyler

Language consultant: Marlynne Grant
BSc, CertEd, MEdPsych, PhD, AFBPs, CPsychol

There is a little yellow duck to find on every page.

First published in 2006 by Usborne Publishing Ltd., Usborne House, 83-85 Saffron Hill, London EC1N 8RT, England. www.usborne.com
Copyright © 2006, 2001 Usborne Publishing Ltd.

Hen has new pens.

She has ten
new pens.

3

"When will you use your
new pens, Hen?"

"Now, Brown
Cow!"

"What will you draw?"

"Straw...

5

... and the big blue sky,
and a yellow bird flying by."

"And zigzags are better than ALL the rest."

Hen hops off her nest.

She zigs and zags from left to right.

"Drawing patterns is
what I like best."

7   8

... until her paper
has run out.

"What can I draw on now?" she shouts.

She zigs and zags all day and night...

"Draw on your eggs!" says Brown Cow.

9　　10

"Draw big dots on your eggs."
"Or more zigzags?" Hen begs.

Hen's zigzags are very bright indeed.

"Zigzags are just what ALL eggs need!"

...if I zigzag all the eggs I find."

"I'm sure the others will not mind...

Now all the eggs are in a dreadful mix.

13   14

Sorting them out
is hard to fix.

15

Hen has made a bad mistake.
That's not her chick.

It's a baby snake!

Usborne
Phonics Readers
Fox on a box

Phil Roxbee Cox
Illustrated by Stephen Cartwright
Edited by Jenny Tyler

Language consultant: Marlynne Grant
BSc, CertEd, MEdPsych, PhD, AFBPs, CPsychol

There is a little yellow duck to find on every page.

First published in 2006 by Usborne Publishing Ltd., Usborne House, 83-85 Saffron Hill, London EC1N 8RT, England. www.usborne.com
Copyright © 2006, 2003 Usborne Publishing Ltd.

Hungry Fox spots
a box.

...a peach!

SPLAT!

PRIZE

Hungry Fox
hops onto
the box.

He tries to reach...

Hungry Fox pushes the box.

"Now I'm as tall as the wall!" calls Fox.

5

SPLAT!

6

"I need honey from the honey bees!" says Fox.

Hungry Fox
pushes the
box.

7

8

SPLAT!

"I want fishes,"
wishes Fox.

Hungry Fox sits on the box.

But a tug from Duck
means he's out
of luck.

SPLAT!

Hungry Fox
is on the box.

11

"I can reach the cooling pies!" cries Fox.

12

But Pup and
Fat Cat ...

...put a stop to that.

13

Hungry Fox falls
into the box.

...to find
cream on
his snout.

He heaves
himself out...

"I'm back in the box!"

shouts Happy Fox.

Usborne
Phonics Readers
Fat cat on a mat

Phil Roxbee Cox
Illustrated by Stephen Cartwright
Edited by Jenny Tyler

Language consultant: Marlynne Grant
BSc, CertEd, MEdPsych, PhD, AFBPs, CPsychol

There is a little yellow duck to spot in every picture.

First published in 2006 by Usborne Publishing Ltd., Usborne House, 83-85 Saffron Hill, London EC1N 8RT, England. www.usborne.com
Copyright © 2006, 1999 Usborne Publishing Ltd.

Fat Cat sees a bee.

BUZZ

Fat Cat flees up a tree.
"I don't like bees!" yelps Fat Cat.

3

"I don't like bees and I don't like trees."

"I don't like bees *or* trees."

"Are you stuck?"
shouts Big Pig.

"Bad luck!" shouts Big Pig.

5

Fat Cat
groans.

"I am stuck.
It *is* bad luck,"
she moans.

The tree bends...

...and the
nest drops
off the end.

The nest drops,
with a plop, on
top of Big Pig.

"Like my new hat, Fat Cat?"

7   8

"Good catch!"
yelps Fat Cat.

Fat Cat lands in a sandy patch.
"I must help the eggs to hatch."

9

Next day,

Fat Cat will
not play.

"Play with me!" says Big Pig.

"Not today," says Fat Cat on her mat.

"Bake a cake with me,"
says Jake Snake.

"Not today," says Fat Cat on her mat.

"Let's run in the sun for fun," says Ted.

"Not today," says Fat Cat on her mat.

"You are lazy," says Big Pig.
"You are crazy," says Jake Snake.

"You are no fun," says Ted.

She hops up
off her mat.

"It's the eggs
from the nest!"
says Big Pig.

"See the
chicks hatch."

"Shh!" says
Fat Cat.

"Stay away,"
says Fat Cat.

Clever Fat Cat!

Usborne
Phonics Readers
Big pig on a dig

Phil Roxbee Cox
Illustrated by Stephen Cartwright
Edited by Jenny Tyler

Language consultant: Marlynne Grant
BSc, CertEd, MEdPsych, PhD, AFBPs, CPsychol

There is a little yellow duck to spot in every picture.

First published in 2006 by Usborne Publishing Ltd., Usborne House, 83-85 Saffron Hill, London EC1N 8RT, England. www.usborne.com
Copyright © 2006, 1999 Usborne Publishing Ltd.

Big Pig gets a letter.

Look for this hat.

Big Pig

Big Pig sees the hat.

There is a map in the hat.

Big Pig runs
to Fat Cat.

4

"Fat Cat! Look at the map in this hat."

"It shows where to dig, Fat Cat."

dig

Map

"Where to dig?
Dig for what,
Big Pig?"

"Gold!" grunts Big Pig.
"Old gold."

5   6

"But I am a cat.
Cats need to nap.
I am a napping cat."

"You dig, Big Pig.
Be a pig on a dig."

7

"Let me nap

and dream of cream."

8

Big Pig sees three green trees.

Big Pig sees three green trees on the map.

9

Big Pig is happy.

He pops on a wig.

Big Pig is happy.

He hops on a twig. He can go on a dig!

"I am a happy big pig on a dig."

"I dig down

and down

and... down."

What has Big Pig found...

...down in the ground?

13   14

It's Funny Bunny.

"There's no old gold here."

Fat Cat grins.

"I drew the map for fun," she says.

Big Pig grins. "Digging is fun too!"

Usborne
Phonics Readers
Frog on a log

Phil Roxbee Cox

Illustrated by Stephen Cartwright

Edited by Jenny Tyler

Language consultant: Marlynne Grant

BSc, CertEd, MEdPsych, PhD, AFBPs, CPsychol

There is a little yellow duck to find on every page.

First published in 2006 by Usborne Publishing Ltd., Usborne House, 83-85 Saffron Hill, London EC1N 8RT, England. www.usborne.com
Copyright © 2006, 2001 Usborne Publishing Ltd.

Frog sits on his log
by the bog.

With one big hop,
he jumps over
the bog.

3

Off he goes! Frog likes to jog.

"I'm a jogging frog
from the log
by the bog."

5

Frog's jogging has ended.
It is foggy.

Out of the fog
runs Pup the dog.

Frog falls off
into the bog.

"You silly dog!"

Pup can't see.

He bumps into Frog's log.

Frog is back up on his log. Along trots Big Pig in the fog.

7   8

...and Frog falls off into the bog.

"You silly hog!"

Pig is looking for
Pup the dog.

Now he bumps into Frog's log...

Next day, it is sunny.

9   10

"Bump into my log!" says Frog.

Is Frog trying to be funny?

"Bump your log!"
barks Pup the dog.

"You will not call us silly dog and hog?"

"No, bump away!" croaks grinning Frog. "I cannot fall off. I'm strapped to my log."

So Big Pig and Pup the dog
bump into the log...

...which tips back into the bog...

...taking with it foolish Frog. 15

Frog is agog.

"Now it is me who is silly. A silly frog!"

Usborne
Phonics Readers
Goose on the loose

Phil Roxbee Cox

Illustrated by Stephen Cartwright

Edited by Jenny Tyler

Language consultant: Marlynne Grant
BSc, CertEd, MEdPstch, PhD, AFBPs, CPsychol

There is a little yellow duck to find on every page.

First published in 2006 by Usborne Publishing Ltd., Usborne House, 83–85 Saffron Hill, London EC1N 8RT, England. www.usborne.com
Copyright © 2006, 2001 Usborne Publishing Ltd.

Goose is on a scooter.
She can't stay and play.

She's a goose on the loose.
"Get out of my way!"

HONK!

She almost runs down Rooster Ron.

"Get out of my way!"
Goose goes scooting on.

HONK!
HONK!

Goose is scooting to Ted's shed...

Ted ends up in his flower bed.

"Look out, behind you.
Watch out, Ted!"

Goose goes scooting down the road.

Toad groans and drops a
heavy load.

GROAN!

She almost scoots
right into Toad.

The cows all moo.

The doves all coo.

The brown owl says,
"too-wit-too-woo".

Now Goose is heading for...

HONK
HONK!

Look out! Goose is on the loose.

She upsets a bunch of kangaroos...

11   12

...and shocks a flock of cockatoos.

There are shouts of "hiss!"
and shouts of "boo!"

Then snarls and howls
and a hullabaloo.

"Goose must be stopped! What shall we do?"

But Goose has stopped, and feels a fool.

She's landed in the penguin pool!

Underpants
for Ants

Russell Punter
Illustrated by Fred Blunt

Nan sells fancy fans and lamps,

hand bells,

clam shells,

pans and stamps.

But customers just stay away.

And so she sits and knits all day.

One cold night, Nan lights a candle

and grabs a small pan by the handle.

But as she pours soup from a can...

a gang of ants leaps from the pan.

"I can help you," Nan declares.

"I have yards of yarn to spare.

I'll knit you something warm to wear."

Nan's whiskers twitch.
Her needles click.

"Handmade underpants!"
"How grand."

Soon bugs are hopping up the hill.

Nan's shop is full, and so's her till.

Nan gets a snug hug from the ants.

"Thanks for our wonderful underpants!"

About phonics

Phonics is a method of teaching reading, used extensively in today's schools. At its heart is an emphasis on identifying the *sounds* of letters, or combinations of letters, that are then put together to make words. These sounds are known as phonemes.

Starting to read

Learning to read is an important milestone for any child. The process can begin well before children start to learn letters and put them together to read words. The sooner children can discover books and enjoy stories and language, the better they will be prepared for reading themselves, first with the help of an adult and then independently.

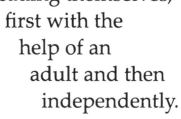

You can find out more about phonics on the Usborne Very First Reading website, **www.usborne.com/veryfirstreading** (US readers go to **www.veryfirstreading.com**). Click on the **Parents** tab at the top of the page, then scroll down and click on **About synthetic phonics**.

Phonemic awareness

An important early stage in pre-reading and early reading is developing phonemic awareness: that is, listening out for the sounds within words. Rhymes, rhyming stories and alliteration are excellent ways of encouraging phonemic awareness.

In this story, your child will soon identify the *a* sound, as in **hand** and **lamps**. Look out, too, for rhymes such as **spare** – **wear** and **thick** – **pick**.

Hearing your child read

If your child is reading a story to you, don't rush to correct mistakes, but be ready to prompt or guide if he or she is struggling. Above all, give plenty of praise and encouragement.

Edited by Jenny Tyler and Lesley Sims

Designed by Caroline Spatz

Reading consultants: Alison Kelly and Anne Washtell

First published in 2013 by Usborne Publishing Ltd., Usborne House, 83-85 Saffron Hill, London EC1N 8RT, England.
www.usborne.com Copyright © 2013 Usborne Publishing Ltd.

Croc gets a shock

Mairi Mackinnon
Illustrated by Fred Blunt

Knock knock. "Who's there?"

"Hey, wake up, Croc!"

"I'm late! And there's so much to do –

I need new shoes, a new bag too.
I'm due at The Zoo at twenty to two."

Croc gulps her breakfast,

grabs her stuff.

She runs, but she's not quick enough.
"I've missed the bus!" She's out of puff.

Hic

Now Croc's in town. "It can't be true!"
The shoe store door says CLOSED TILL 2.

She sighs. "These boots will have to do."

It's party time! The Zoo looks fine.
The lions and rhinos wait in line.

THE ZOO CAFE

Happy Birthday Croc!

The hippos hold a birthday sign.
But where is Croc?

"We'll have to wait. She's always late."

"At last! Come on, let's celebrate!"

Croc swallows quickly.
"What's up, Croc?"

"Unwrap your presents, Croc."
Croc picks a box...

...and gets a shock.
"CUCKOO! CUCKOO!"

"My gosh! I almost dropped the box."

"You've never seen a cuckoo clock?"

"It's a tip-top tick-tock cuckoo clock!"

About phonics

Phonics is a method of teaching reading, used extensively in today's schools. At its heart is an emphasis on identifying the *sounds* of letters, or combinations of letters, that are then put together to make words. These sounds are known as phonemes.

Starting to read

Learning to read is an important milestone for any child. The process can begin well before children start to learn letters and put them together to read words. The sooner children can discover books and enjoy stories and language, the better they will be prepared for reading themselves, first with the help of an adult and then independently.

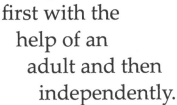

You can find out more about phonics on the Usborne Very First Reading website, **www.usborne.com/veryfirstreading** (US readers go to **www.veryfirstreading.com**). Click on the **Parents** tab at the top of the page, then scroll down and click on **About synthetic phonics**.

Phonemic awareness

An important early stage in pre-reading and early reading is developing phonemic awareness: that is, listening out for the sounds within words. Rhymes, rhyming stories and alliteration are excellent ways of encouraging phonemic awareness.

In this story, your child will soon identify the *o* sound, as in **Croc** and **clock** or in **stopped** or **what**. Look out, too, for rhymes such as **due** – **Zoo** and **fine** – **sign**.

Hearing your child read

If your child is reading a story to you, don't rush to correct mistakes, but be ready to prompt or guide if he or she is struggling. Above all, give plenty of praise and encouragement.

Edited by Jenny Tyler and Lesley Sims

Designed by Caroline Spatz

Reading consultants: Alison Kelly and Anne Washtell
University of Roehampton

First published in 2013 by Usborne Publishing Ltd., Usborne House, 83-85 Saffron Hill, London EC1N 8RT, England.
www.usborne.com Copyright © 2013 Usborne Publishing Ltd.

Bee makes tea

Lesley Sims

Illustrated by Fred Blunt

Meet Bee.

Bee lives
beside the sea.

Today she's all a-flutter, for it's Queen Bee's birthday tea.

Bee buzzes home
and starts to bake.

Soon her rooms fill up with cake.

Chocolate cheesecakes on the chairs...

Cherry cupcakes
up the stairs...

Pies piled high with
plums and pears.

Ant runs in and grins with glee.
"You're making tea!"

For my Queen Bee.

"Her birthday tea is by the sea."

They stack up cups and fill the pot.
Bee starts to frown. It looks a lot.

He finds his friends and lines them up.

They carry cakes and plates and cups.

Two take the milk.
Three take the pot.

"Look out!"
calls Bee.

That tea
is hot.

"Wow!" says Ant.
"That cake is tall."

"Speed up!" shouts Ant.
"Move that cake faster."

Then one ant slips and trips...
Disaster!

"Oh no!" Bee cries.
She sobs and sighs.

That *was* my Queen Bee's big surprise.

"The Queen will be so mad with me.
She'll say that I'm a bad, bad bee."

"Collect it all," Ant tells his team.
"Now quick, Bee!
Whip some buttercream."

"You need to use the cream like glue...
See? Stuck together, good as new."

The Queen Bee gasps and laughs,
"Hee, hee! A special cake
that looks like me?"

"Thank you for my birthday tea!"

About phonics

Phonics is a method of teaching reading used extensively in today's schools. At its heart is an emphasis on identifying the *sounds* of letters, or combinations of letters, that are then put together to make words. These sounds are known as phonemes.

Starting to read
Learning to read is an important milestone for any child. The process can begin well before children start to learn letters and put them together to read words. The sooner children can discover books and enjoy stories and language, the better they will be prepared for reading themselves, first with the help of an adult and then independently.

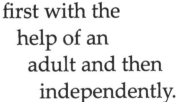

You can find out more about phonics on the Usborne Very First Reading website, **www.usborne.com/veryfirstreading** (US readers go to **www.veryfirstreading.com**). Click on the **Parents** tab at the top of the page, then scroll down and click on **About synthetic phonics**.

Phonemic awareness

An important early stage in pre-reading and early reading is developing phonemic awareness: that is, listening out for the sounds within words. Rhymes, rhyming stories and alliteration are excellent ways of encouraging phonemic awareness.

In this story, your child will soon identify the *ee* sound, as in **bee** and **tea** or **queen** or **team**. Look out, too, for rhymes such as **chairs** – **stairs** and **sighs** – **surprise**.

Hearing your child read

If your child is reading a story to you, don't rush to correct mistakes, but be ready to prompt or guide if he or she is struggling. Above all, do give plenty of praise and encouragement.

Edited by Jenny Tyler
Designed by Caroline Spatz

Reading consultants: Alison Kelly and Anne Washtell

First published in 2013 by Usborne Publishing Ltd., Usborne House, 83-85 Saffron Hill, London EC1N 8RT, England.
www.usborne.com Copyright © 2013 Usborne Publishing Ltd.

Bug in a rug

Russell Punter

Illustrated by David Semple

"I need my sleep tonight,"
says Bug.

"Tomorrow I start work for Slug."

Bug glugs hot
chocolate from
a mug.

Then snuggles
up inside
his rug.

Bug hugs his bear.
He starts to nap.

Then he hears barking...

Loud party music
shakes the wall.

Below, a baby starts to bawl.

Bug plugs his ears,

but all too soon...

A car alarm adds to the row.

He plods to work at Slug's Rug Store.

"I feel so sleepy now," thinks Bug.

"And all these rugs look soft and snug..."

When Slug comes back
at ten o'clock...

About phonics

Phonics is a method of teaching reading used extensively in today's schools. At its heart is an emphasis on identifying the *sounds* of letters, or combinations of letters, that are then put together to make words. These sounds are known as phonemes.

Starting to read

Learning to read is an important milestone for any child. The process can begin well before children start to learn letters and put them together to read words. The sooner children can discover books and enjoy stories and language, the better they will be prepared for reading themselves, first with the help of an adult and then independently.

You can find out more about phonics on the Usborne Very First Reading website, **www.usborne.com/veryfirstreading** (US readers go to **www.veryfirstreading.com**). Click on the **Parents** tab at the top of the page, then scroll down and click on **About synthetic phonics**.

Phonemic awareness

An important early stage in pre-reading and early reading is developing phonemic awareness: that is, listening out for the sounds within words. Rhymes, rhyming stories and alliteration are excellent ways of encouraging phonemic awareness.

In this story, your child will soon identify the *u* sound, as in **bug** and **rug**. Look out, too, for rhymes such as **wall** – **bawl** and **nap** – **yap**.

Hearing your child read

If your child is reading a story to you, don't rush to correct mistakes, but be ready to prompt or guide if he or she is struggling. Above all, do give plenty of praise and encouragement.

Edited by Jenny Tyler and Lesley Sims
Designed by Sam Whibley

Reading consultants: Alison Kelly and Anne Washtell

First published in 2015 by Usborne Publishing Ltd., Usborne House, 83-85 Saffron Hill, London EC1N 8RT, England.
www.usborne.com Copyright © 2015 Usborne Publishing Ltd.

Cow takes a bow

Russell Punter

Illustrated by Fred Blunt

Today the circus is in town.

Brown Cow sets out
to track it down.

Here comes the boss.
Cow sees him frown.

"I'll help," says Cow.

"Just show me how."

Cow slips and trips.

She tries some tricks...

...but drops the pies,

and spills the bricks.

Her tricycle just spins around.

Her trumpet makes a silly sound.

Her juggling balls all hit the ground.

Her hat flies off.

Her pants fall down.

"It's all gone wrong!"
Brown Cow flops down.

Now she's the one who wears a frown.

"I'm sorry I messed up!" howls Cow.

"Listen!" he says.

The crowd shouts, "Wow!"

Cow takes a bow.

About phonics

Phonics is a method of teaching reading which is used extensively in today's schools. At its heart is an emphasis on identifying the *sounds* of letters, or combinations of letters, that are then put together to make words. These sounds are known as phonemes.

Starting to read
Learning to read is an important milestone for any child. The process can begin well before children start to learn letters and put them together to read words. The sooner children can discover books and enjoy stories and language, the better they will be prepared for reading themselves, first with the help of an adult and then independently.

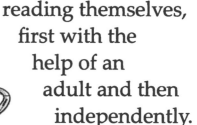

You can find out more about phonics on the Usborne Very First Reading website, **www.usborne.com/veryfirstreading** (US readers go to **www.veryfirstreading.com**). Click on the **Parents** tab at the top of the page, then scroll down and click on **About synthetic phonics**.

Phonemic awareness

An important early stage in pre-reading and early reading is developing phonemic awareness: that is, listening out for the sounds within words. Rhymes, rhyming stories and alliteration are excellent ways of encouraging phonemic awareness.

In this story, your child will soon identify the *ow* sound, as in **Brown Cow** or in **around** or **ground**. Look out, too, for rhymes such as **today** – **hooray** and **slips** – **trips**.

Hearing your child read

If your child is reading a story to you, don't rush to correct mistakes, but be ready to prompt or guide if he or she is struggling. Above all, do give plenty of praise and encouragement.

Edited by Jenny Tyler, Lesley Sims and Mairi Mackinnon

Designed by Caroline Spatz

First published in 2013 by Usborne Publishing Ltd., Usborne House, 83-85 Saffron Hill, London EC1N 8RT, England.
www.usborne.com Copyright © 2013 Usborne Publishing Ltd.

Snail brings the mail

Russell Punter
and Mairi Mackinnon

Illustrated by Fred Blunt

Hooray for Snail! He brings the mail.

Day in, day out, he will not fail.

A box
for Fox,

and three
for Bee.

From dawn to dusk, Snail's on the go.

He does work hard, but he's so slow.

His friends may
have to wait all day.

"Poor Snail. He does his best," they say.

One morning, things go wrong for Snail.

He wakes up late.

He drops the mail.

It starts to rain. It starts to hail.

Snail won't give up.

The cold wind blows – it's quite a gale.

The sky turns dark,

and Snail turns pale.

The road is flooded.
Bad luck, Snail.

He can't get through.
Snail wails, "I've failed."

But look! A tractor – up for sale!

The deal is done. Now watch Snail go!

He won't get stuck in rain or snow.

These days, the mail
is right on time.

And Snail gets through,

come rain or shine.

About phonics

Phonics is a method of teaching reading, used extensively in today's schools. At its heart is an emphasis on identifying the *sounds* of letters, or combinations of letters, that are then put together to make words. These sounds are known as phonemes.

Starting to read

Learning to read is an important milestone for any child. The process can begin well before children start to learn letters and put them together to read words. The sooner children can discover books and enjoy stories and language, the better they will be prepared for reading themselves, first with the help of an adult and then independently.

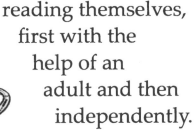

You can find out more about phonics on the Usborne Very First Reading website, **www.usborne.com/veryfirstreading** (US readers go to **www.veryfirstreading.com**). Click on the **Parents** tab at the top of the page, then scroll down and click on **About synthetic phonics**.

Phonemic awareness

An important early stage in pre-reading and early reading is developing phonemic awareness: that is, listening out for the sounds within words. Rhymes, rhyming stories and alliteration are excellent ways of encouraging phonemic awareness.

In this story, your child will soon identify the *ai* sound, as in **Snail** and **Mail** or in **wait** or **day**. Look out, too, for rhymes such as **fox** – **box** and **bee** – **three**.

Hearing your child read

If your child is reading a story to you, don't rush to correct mistakes, but be ready to prompt or guide if he or she is struggling. Above all, give plenty of praise and encouragement.

Edited by Jenny Tyler and Lesley Sims

Designed by Caroline Spatz

Reading consultants: Alison Kelly and Anne Washtell
University of Roehampton

First published in 2013 by Usborne Publishing Ltd., Usborne House, 83-85 Saffron Hill, London EC1N 8RT, England.
www.usborne.com Copyright © 2013 Usborne Publishing Ltd.

Crow in the snow

Lesley Sims

Illustrated by Fred Blunt

Crow is flying over snow.

He spies some paw prints far below.

"Ho, ho," says Crow
and swoops down low.

"I think I'll follow where they go."

Crow starts hopping to and fro.

He picks up sticks,
    some stones and cones...

And look –
a crow made out of snow.

Crow blinks and sees the trail
goes on. "What next?" he thinks
and trots along.

He spots a red
sled by a gate,

a yellow
hat,

a fallen
skate.

The trail leads to...

...a frozen lake.

Creak!

Mice and voles
and Mole are skating.

"Oh no!" cries Crow.
"The ice is breaking."

Crack!

"Help!" calls Mole. "I'm falling in. I'm all cold and I can't swim."

Crow flies fast.

He leaves the lake.
In seconds, he's flown past the gate.

He spies the snowmen, dives down low,
grabs a scarf and back he goes.

With one last heave, cold Mole is free.
He sits and shivers by a tree.

"Let me get the sled," says Crow...

and soon he's giving Mole a tow.

Now all are warm and safe and snug.
Mole gives a grin and lifts his mug.

"A toast," he says. "A toast to Crow. He's the hero of the snow!"

About phonics

Phonics is a method of teaching reading, used extensively in today's schools. At its heart is an emphasis on identifying the *sounds* of letters, or combinations of letters, that are then put together to make words. These sounds are known as phonemes.

Starting to read
Learning to read is an important milestone for any child. The process can begin well before children start to learn letters and put them together to read words. The sooner children can discover books and enjoy stories and language, the better they will be prepared for reading themselves, first with the help of an adult and then independently.

You can find out more about phonics on the Usborne Very First Reading website, **www.usborne.com/veryfirstreading** (US readers go to **www.veryfirstreading.com**). Click on the **Parents** tab at the top of the page, then scroll down and click on **About synthetic phonics**.

Phonemic awareness

An important early stage in pre-reading and early reading is developing phonemic awareness: that is, listening out for the sounds within words. Rhymes, rhyming stories and alliteration are excellent ways of encouraging phonemic awareness.

In this story, your child will soon identify the *o* sound, as in **crow** and **snow** or **stone** or **mole**. Look out, too, for rhymes such as **red** – **sled** and **gate** – **skate**.

Hearing your child read

If your child is reading a story to you, don't rush to correct mistakes, but be ready to prompt or guide if he or she is struggling. Above all, do give plenty of praise and encouragement.

Edited by Jenny Tyler
Designed by Caroline Spatz
Additional design by Sam Chandler

Reading consultants: Alison Kelly and Anne Washtell

First published in 2013 by Usborne Publishing Ltd., Usborne House, 83-85 Saffron Hill, London EC1N 8RT, England.
www.usborne.com Copyright © 2013 Usborne Publishing Ltd.

Goat in a boat

Lesley Sims

Illustrated by David Semple

"If I hook a fish, or two...

Cook can cook a fishy stew."

"I'll go for a row with Stoat," thinks Goat.

Stoat's room is bare.
There's no one there.

"Oh look! He wrote a note," says Goat.

Goat rows his boat around the moat.

He sits and gazes
at his float.

It sinks. He blinks.
"A fish!" he thinks.

He lifts his rod...

That's odd. It clinks.

Then Goat
spots Stoat.

Hop in
the boat!

They hear a noise among the trees.
Is it the breeze? The scared friends freeze.

An army!
Stoat has shaking knees.

But poor Stoat has a sore, sore throat.
He can't shout out along with Goat.

The castle soldiers do not hear.

Then Goat hits on a clever plan.
They bash his catch...

CLASH! CLATTER! CLANG!

The lookout hears. He gives a cry.
The drawbridge rises to the sky.

The army
can't get in.
They flee.

Goat and Stoat
row home for tea.

Goat sighs. "I have no fish for Cook."

"You do," croaks Stoat.
"Just take a look!"

About phonics

Phonics is a method of teaching reading used extensively in today's schools. At its heart is an emphasis on identifying the *sounds* of letters, or combinations of letters, that are then put together to make words. These sounds are known as phonemes.

Starting to read
Learning to read is an important milestone for any child. The process can begin well before children start to learn letters and put them together to read words. The sooner children can discover books and enjoy stories and language, the better they will be prepared for reading themselves, first with the help of an adult and then independently.

You can find out more about phonics on the Usborne Very First Reading website, **www.usborne.com/veryfirstreading** (US readers go to **www.veryfirstreading.com**). Click on the **Parents** tab at the top of the page, then scroll down and click on **About synthetic phonics**.

Phonemic awareness

An important early stage in pre-reading and early reading is developing phonemic awareness: that is, listening out for the sounds within words. Rhymes, rhyming stories and alliteration are excellent ways of encouraging phonemic awareness.

In this story, your child will soon identify the *oa* sound, as in **goat** and **boat**. Look out, too, for rhymes such as **sinks** – **blinks** and **cry** – **sky**.

Hearing your child read

If your child is reading a story to you, don't rush to correct mistakes, but be ready to prompt or guide if he or she is struggling. Above all, do give plenty of praise and encouragement.

Edited by Jenny Tyler
Designed by Sam Whibley

Reading consultants: Alison Kelly and Anne Washtell

First published in 2015 by Usborne Publishing Ltd., Usborne House, 83-85 Saffron Hill, London EC1N 8RT, England.
www.usborne.com Copyright © 2015 Usborne Publishing Ltd.

Llamas in pyjamas

Russell Punter

Illustrated by David Semple

Sam, Ali and Charlie
all yell with delight.

Please come to my
sleepover.

Frankie

There's a creepy sleepover
at Frankie's tonight.

They pick out pyjamas
with stripes...

spots...

and dots.

With their packs on their backs,
off to Frankie's they trot.

Into Frankie's big bedroom
run three jolly llamas.

Charlie's look silly.

And Frankie's are blue.

They play games by torchlight.

"Woo-hoo!" Frankie wails.

"Let's stay up till midnight,
and tell spooky tales."

They whisper of spirits that shiver and shake,

and quivering monsters,

until it's so late...

...they fall fast asleep,

but wake with a jump.

"Take cover!" calls Frankie.
"Or he'll eat us all."

BUMP! BUMP!
CLUNK! CLANK!

They hide under blankets
and slide to the floor.

CREAK! goes the door.
It opens a crack.

In creeps...

...Frankie's grandma
with a great midnight snack.

About phonics

Phonics is a method of teaching reading which is used extensively in today's schools. At its heart is an emphasis on identifying the *sounds* of letters, or combinations of letters, that are then put together to make words. These sounds are known as phonemes.

Starting to read

Learning to read is an important milestone for any child. The process can begin well before children start to learn letters and put them together to read words. The sooner children can discover books and enjoy stories and language, the better they will be prepared for reading themselves, first with the help of an adult and then independently.

You can find out more about phonics on the Usborne Very First Reading website, **www.usborne.com/veryfirstreading**. Click on the **Parents** tab at the top of the page, then scroll down and click on **About synthetic phonics**.

Phonemic awareness

An important early stage in pre-reading and early reading is developing phonemic awareness: that is, listening out for the sounds within words. Rhymes, rhyming stories and alliteration are excellent ways of encouraging phonemic awareness.

In this story, your child will soon identify the *ll* sound, as in **call** and **jolly**. Look out, too, for rhymes such as **spots** – **dots** and **jump** – **thump**.

Hearing your child read

If your child is reading a story to you, don't rush to correct mistakes, but be ready to prompt or guide if he or she is struggling. Above all, do give plenty of praise and encouragement.

Edited by Jenny Tyler and Lesley Sims
Designed by Sam Whibley

First published in 2014 by Usborne Publishing Ltd., Usborne House, 83-85 Saffron Hill, London EC1N 8RT, England.
www.usborne.com Copyright © 2014 Usborne Publishing Ltd.

Raccoon on the moon

Russell Punter

Illustrated by David Semple

"Goodbye!" cries Raccoon.
"I'm off to the moon.

I'll be back by lunchtime,
or late afternoon."

Goose grins and she giggles.

You foolish Raccoon!

3, 2, 1...

BOOM!

He zooms into space.

Far up to the stars,
at a fabulous pace.

He reaches the moon.
But SMASH! What a shock.

His craft crashes BUMP
on a sharp lump of rock.

The ship hits the ground.
It's split down one side.

Now I might be stuck here.

Raccoon bounds
outside...

"My name is Zack. I live on the moon.

Give me your hand and
I'll have you back soon."

Zip's buggy chugs up.

He whips out a tool.

Fizz! goes his gizmo.

The ship is fixed.

climb mountains...

see valleys...

until, three
hours later...

The ship
reaches Earth.

"Three cheers for Raccoon!"

His chums greet their hero.

You've been
to the moon!

About phonics

Phonics is a method of teaching reading used extensively in today's schools. At its heart is an emphasis on identifying the *sounds* of letters, or combinations of letters, that are then put together to make words. These sounds are known as phonemes.

Starting to read
Learning to read is an important milestone for any child. The process can begin well before children start to learn letters and put them together to read words. The sooner children can discover books and enjoy stories and language, the better they will be prepared for reading themselves, first with the help of an adult and then independently.

You can find out more about phonics on the Usborne Very First Reading website, **www.usborne.com/veryfirstreading** (US readers go to **www.veryfirstreading.com**). Click on the **Parents** tab at the top of the page, then scroll down and click on **About synthetic phonics**.

Phonemic awareness

An important early stage in pre-reading and early reading is developing phonemic awareness: that is, listening out for the sounds within words. Rhymes, rhyming stories and alliteration are excellent ways of encouraging phonemic awareness.

In this story, your child will soon identify the *oo* sound, as in **soon** and **zoom**. Look out, too, for rhymes such as **bump** – **lump** and **high** – **cry**.

Hearing your child read

If your child is reading a story to you, don't rush to correct mistakes, but be ready to prompt or guide if he or she is struggling. Above all, do give plenty of praise and encouragement.

Edited by Jenny Tyler and Lesley Sims
Designed by Sam Whibley

Reading consultants: Alison Kelly and Anne Washtell

First published in 2015 by Usborne Publishing Ltd., Usborne House, 83-85 Saffron Hill, London EC1N 8RT, England.
www.usborne.com Copyright © 2015 Usborne Publishing Ltd.